ITALIAN PAINTING
UP TO LEONARDO AND RAPHAEL

" Discussions on Art "

BRITISH PAINTING (*From Hogarth's Day to Ours*) by William Gaunt
FRENCH PAINTING (*From the 17th Century to To-day*) by T. W. Earp
DUTCH PAINTING by J. B. Manson
FLEMISH PAINTING by Emile Cammaerts
ITALIAN PAINTING (*Up to Leonardo and Raphael*) by Tancred Borenius
LATER ITALIAN PAINTING (*From Titian to Tiepolo*) by Tancred Borenius
SPANISH PAINTING by Philip Hendy
MODERN PAINTING by Reginald Brill

THE LAMENTATION OVER THE DEAD CHRIST *by Giotto* (1266/76-1337)

ITALIAN PAINTING

UP TO LEONARDO AND RAPHAEL

TANCRED BORENIUS

DURNING-LAWRENCE PROFESSOR OF THE HISTORY OF ART
IN THE UNIVERSITY OF LONDON

WITH 36 PLATES IN COLOUR & MONOCHROME

AVALON PRESS: AND COLLINS

FIRST PUBLISHED 1945 BY AVALON PRESS, LTD., AND THE CENTRAL INSTITUTE
OF ART AND DESIGN, AND DISTRIBUTED BY WM. COLLINS SONS AND CO., LTD.,
14 ST. JAMES'S PLACE, LONDON, S.W.I.   REVISED EDITION 1946

TEXT PRINTED IN GREAT BRITAIN BY RICHARD CLAY AND COMPANY, LTD., BUNGAY, SUFFOLK
COLOUR PLATES BY WATERLOW AND SONS, LTD., LONDON AND DUNSTABLE, AND FINE ART
ENGRAVERS, LTD., ESHER. PHOTOGRAVURE BY L. T. A. ROBINSON, LTD., LONDON, S.W. 9

ITALIAN PAINTING

CHAPTER I

THE passing of Imperial Rome and the calamities entailed thereby inevitably had a powerful effect upon the fortunes of art in Italy; but at no time did art come to a complete standstill in the peninsula, and even at quite remote periods of the Middle Ages we can trace considerable artistic activity in various parts of Italy. Upon this soil and in this setting the art of the classical, Graeco-Roman age could never completely fade from people's consciousness. At an early period the splendid, semi-oriental art of the Eastern, or Byzantine, Empire also acquired great importance for the development of art in Italy; and her various invaders from the north contributed their quota of tradition to the artistic aspiration which found expression in Italy. All this has to be borne in mind if we want to account for the way in which what we understand by " Italian art " came to be formed.

The object of this book is to give an outline of the history of Italian painting up to Leonardo and Raphael; but at the outset it should be stressed that this survey must notice to some extent Italian architecture and Italian sculpture as well. The interconnection between these three arts has at all times been very close in Italy; in some striking instances we find the practice of all of them united in one person; artists, preeminently known as painters, have been trained under sculptors, and *vice versa*. Some grasp of the conditions that governed Italian architecture and sculpture is indispensable in order to understand the development of Italian painting.

All generalisations contain an element of error; but it has become the universally accepted thesis—and substantially this view is well founded—that the history of Italian painting begins with Giotto, at the end of the thirteenth century. If we make this the working basis of the present enquiry, the proper perspective of art history can, however, only be obtained if we first notice briefly some developments in Italian sculpture which preceded Giotto.

Which is the great individual work that can be singled out, with fair justification, as standing at the head of the history of Italian sculpture? The answer cannot be long in doubt: it is Niccolò Pisano's famous pulpit in the baptistry of Pisa, dating from 1260. Pre-eminently in the six marble bas-reliefs of scenes from the Life of Christ which adorn it we find the most striking use made of a language of artistic expression which is instinct with classical character, without by any means descending to slavish dependence or imitation. The style which we see here is above all marked by staid dignity and simple heroic grandeur; and while we can realise the channels through which this derivation from classical exemplars came about, this pure and noble art has an individual value all its own.

Evidence of a notable evolution is patent in another great pulpit which Niccolò Pisano, with the assistance of a number of pupils, carried out for the Cathedral of Siena only a few years later—between 1265 and 1268. Here the Olympic calm and massive character of form which characterise the Pisa pulpit have given way to greater nervous tension of expression and increased complexity in the handling of the plastic problem. There can be no doubt that this is due to the influence of a current of art which meanwhile had reached the circle of Niccolò Pisano from its country of origin, France—the influence of Gothic art.

The style of Gothic art was the first absolutely complete and consistent style to arise in Europe after that of classical Greece and Rome; and, like that style, the style of Gothic art succeeded in infiltrating into practically every country of what was then the civilised world. We call a church a Gothic church when it combines such features as pointed arches, intersecting ribbed vaultings and flying buttresses; and bearing in mind more especially France, what is characteristic of the Gothic style of architecture—fully developed in that country by the middle of the twelfth century—is, to put it in general terms, the tendency to emphasise the vertical lines, the uprights, to do away with wall space as far as possible and to turn the whole building as it were into a large scaffolding. These tendencies are then also reflected in Gothic painting and sculpture; tall and slender forms predominate, and in later Gothic figure art the long sweeping curves mark a feature of style which is never absent.

Now, though Italy was by no means deaf to the message of Gothic art, yet the system of French Gothic architecture was adopted there only with considerable modifications. Verticalism plays nothing like as important a part in Italy as in France; a sense of spaciousness, inherited from classical architecture, was always present in Italy, and the windows tended to be kept considerably smaller, thereby leaving large spaces of wall for the Italian painters to work upon. The first great sculptor of Italy who unreservedly proclaims his connection with Gothic art is Niccolò Pisano's son, Giovanni Pisano (c. 1245–c. 1315); and these characteristics go hand in hand with the power of dramatic expression of which there is little trace in Niccolò Pisano, whereas it is characteristically Italian, and in Giovanni Pisano at times pro-

vides astonishing anticipations of later developments of Italian art.

The work of Giovanni Pisano, like that of his father, includes two great pulpits. One of them, in the Church of Sant' Andrea at Pistoia, and eminently typical of Giovanni Pisano's individual trend, is the bas-relief of the *Massacre of the Innocents* on one of the faces of this pulpit, with its violence of action in the figures and their intensity in conveying the sense of drama. At the same time, the treatment of form shows how far Giovanni Pisano goes in his adoption of the Gothic system of design.

With Niccolò and Giovanni Pisano the province of Tuscany had achieved a leading position in the development of Italian sculpture—a position which it was to hold for a long period to come. In the work of a younger contemporary of Giovanni Pisano, Giotto † (1266/76–1337), Tuscany also became associated with one of the most glorious developments in the history of Italian painting; though Giotto more particularly ranks as a member of the school of painting of Florence, which, among the cities of Tuscany, only slowly had reached the prominent position in the annals of painting which was eventually to belong to her. An earlier Florentine painter than Giotto is Cimabue (1240?–after 1302), traditionally looked upon as the father of Italian painting, and the master of Giotto. The latter, however, on the evidence of his works, may be regarded, in the first instance, as a scion of the great school of painting which existed in thirteenth-century Rome.

Despite his period, Giotto owes comparatively little to the Gothic: in fact one might describe his art briefly as reflecting classical and Byzantine traditions, as well as evincing a native Italian dramatic instinct and a new power of coming to grips with reality.

Concerning the conditions under which Italian art of the thirteenth century—the *Duecento*, in Italian parlance—developed,

† Frontispiece, Plates 5 and 6

there are one or two points of outstanding importance which here may be noted. The thirteenth century is the period when, from the political point of view, the innumerable Italian municipalities reached the stage of full development, and when an ideal atmosphere for artistic effort was thus created in all these flourishing rival communities. The thirteenth century is also the period when a most remarkable and widespread revival of religious life takes place in Italy, mainly as a result of the influence of St. Francis of Assisi, the great national saint, at once a poet of the highest order, a religious reformer and the founder of an organisation—the Order of the Franciscan Friars—which was to assume gigantic proportions.

Giotto painted several remarkable panel pictures which have come down to us; but it is in his frescoes that the full range and significance of Giotto's art can best be appreciated. There are three great groups of frescoes which above all claim attention: those of the life of St. Francis in the Upper Church of San Francesco at Assisi, which chronologically come first (we may date them roughly between 1295 and 1300); then the frescoes in the Arena Chapel at Padua, which were probably painted in 1303-1305; and finally the frescoes painted by Giotto somewhere about 1320-1330 in two chapels—the Bardi and the Peruzzi Chapels—in the Church of Santa Croce at Florence. In these three groups of frescoes the whole of Giotto's evolution and the essence of his performance lie patent before us.

The Assisi frescoes—lovable and wonderful as they are, and though it is precisely through them that countless friends have been won for the art of Giotto—nevertheless raise a problem at the outset; there is no documentary proof that they are by Giotto. In trying to arrive at a grasp of their true significance and status, we may note, to begin with, that at a time when there existed very elaborate and binding traditions for the treatment of Scriptural scenes, the life of St. Francis, even if it was no stranger to art, had been depicted incomparably less frequently—after all, St. Francis had not been dead so very long when the Assisi series was completed. The choice of the subjects in the latter is, indeed, to a very limited extent dictated by precedent; and the spectator gains the impression of an artist who, free and untrammelled to a large extent, sets out scenes from everyday life around him, with a singular persuasive power, subtlety of observation and dramatic effectiveness in conveying the whole to us.

This is not to say that the St. Francis series is in any way marked by sustained accomplishment. On the contrary, there is much in these frescoes that is definitely primitive—only it is a primitive of genius who speaks to us from them. That there is evidence of several hands in the actual execution is also not to be denied; but that, after all, is in obvious conformity with the conditions under which a great pictorial enterprise like this would be carried out. Links with the art of Giotto are certainly present in plenty; but there is one consideration which weighs particularly heavily; when, late in his life, in his frescoes in the Bardi Chapel at Florence, Giotto treated several of the subjects occurring in the Assisi series, he did it exactly in the way in which an artist of full maturity would handle a subject tried by him before. Hence, although the authorship of Giotto has been insistently questioned in the case of the Assisi frescoes, there is a great deal to be said for regarding them as an early work by him; and for various reasons the date mentioned above—1295-1300—suggests itself as roughly applicable to them.

With the frescoes of the Arena Chapel at Padua we are on absolutely safe ground critically: there is no possibility of doubting that this great picture chronicle of the lives of the Virgin and Christ is by anybody but Giotto, as to whose grasp of massive and simple form it furnishes basic evidence.

Iconographically, Giotto found himself here supplied with no end of precedent : nevertheless there is evidence, upon every step, of freshness of approach and vividness of expression, however close the contact with the traditional past remains. Altogether, it is an artist considerably ripened who meets us here ; and the increase in telling power shown by his compositions leaps to the eye. His essential resource and freedom from convention are strikingly shown by one at first sight insignificant passage in the great fresco of *The Last Judgment*, on the entrance wall of the chapel—the line of the seated Apostles marks a foreshortened curve. This motif Raphael in his fresco of the *Disputà* in the Vatican was to carry to its final consummation.

The trend of evolution marked in the Arena paintings is continued in the Santa Croce frescoes, which, as we saw, were painted about a score of years later and, in fact, not very long before the death of Giotto. They are unfortunately not in very good condition, which is all the more regrettable as they clearly were of paramount importance for the further development of Florentine painting. This much can, however, be deduced, even in their present condition, from these frescoes—and especially from those in the Peruzzi chapel—that they

bequeathed to the Florentine school a tradition of effective rendering of space and form, of monumental dramatic composition and perhaps even of *chiaroscuro*, of which, about a century later, Masaccio, rather than any one of Giotto's immediate successors, became the true heir, pointing the way also to artists of still later ages.

To contend, then, that practically the whole of the development of Italian Renaissance painting is present in Giotto in germ is without doubt to introduce a most important aspect of Giotto's position in the history of art ; but when all is said and done it is, of course, his performance intrinsically and on its own which counts in the final instance. If one were to try to sum up Giotto's greatness in a few words, one might say that it springs from his power of expressing, with a richness and intensity unsurpassed, sentiments which are universal in their appeal, in a form which has all the nobility of Italy and her classical heritage. That the heart of Italy should go out to him is natural and inevitable ; but we may claim that he belongs to the world precisely because, with a great universal genius such as his, transcending all frontiers and nationalities, Giotto never for a moment lets us forget that he is an Italian of Italians : *italianissimo*.

CHAPTER II

THE Florentine school of painting became exceedingly prolific during the fourteenth century (the *Trecento*). In many ways the formula created by Giotto set a pattern for the painters of Florence—indeed, an ascription to him has tended to become a generic label for paintings of this century—although the real development of art along the lines which Giotto first struck out was not to come until later. Altar-pieces of consider-

able size, as well as smaller devotional images, formed one section of this pictorial output ; but even more characteristic of the Florentine school were the frescoes, of which the number is legion, and which sometimes were carried out in imposing cycles.

Among the most gifted of the Florentine painters early in the century was Bernardo Daddi (*c.* 1290–1348) : we possess by him many panel pictures of the Madonna and the

Crucifixion which show his remarkable powers of sensitive silhouetting and, at times, real dramatic expression; and some frescoes by him in the Pucci-Berardi Chapel in Santa Croce—that great museum above all of Florentine fresco painting during the Trecento—bear witness to the same effect. Taddeo Gaddi (c. 1300–1363/66) is said to have served as Giotto's assistant for twenty-four years: without being an artist of genius, he does not lack some solid accomplishment, and he is notable on account of some sporadic attempts to increase the range of painting, so as to suggest effects of illumination breaking the darkness of the night.

A more gifted master is one whom we all know as Maso, and who occupies a position of some distinction in the Florentine school of the middle of the Trecento. His chief claim to fame are the frescoes of the Legend of St. Sylvester which he painted in the Church of Santa Croce. These show considerable gifts of composition as well as of the imaginative use of landscape; there is also much expression and sensitiveness in his heads and poses.

An impressive performance is to be associated with the painter Andrea Bonaiuti, who in 1365 undertook to decorate with frescoes the chapter-house of the Church of Santa Maria Novella. These frescoes still exist, and have achieved much popularity from being described at some length by John Ruskin in his *Mornings in Florence*. The whole is a somewhat lifeless performance, setting out an exceedingly cumbrous allegory, of which the glorification of the Dominican Order plays an important part; but of the magnificent decorative effect of the whole there is no doubt.

A prolific artist of the second half of the Trecento—he died in 1396—is Agnolo Gaddi, the son of Taddeo Gaddi. He is perhaps specially memorable on account of the way in which certain of his frescoes carry out a particular method of depicting a story. The method in question, known as the " method

of continuous representation," and causing the successive incidents of a story to be set out alongside of one another, had a long ancestry in art. Giotto, though he occasionally used it, did not favour it, but it came to the fore in subsequent Trecento painting in Florence, and Agnolo Gaddi carried it to perfectly absurd lengths; as witness some of his frescoes in the choir of Santa Croce at Florence, where the jumble of juxtaposed incidents succeeds in making the whole entirely unintelligible to an onlooker not specially primed.

The list of these Trecento painters of Florence could be easily lengthened, but some idea has been given of artistic personalities and general tendencies. We may therefore turn to the consideration of the early history of a notable school of painting which existed in another city of Tuscany—Siena.

Contrary to the school of painting in Rome, which came to a sudden end as a result of the disasters which overtook the Eternal City at the beginning of the fourteenth century, the Sienese school, which first acquired real importance at the end of the Duecento, was to experience a long lease of unbroken life. The great master who raised it to outstanding significance was Duccio di Buoninsigna (c. 1260–1319), a slightly older contemporary of Giotto's; and he indicates the direction which in its essentials was to be pursued for generations by the Sienese school. Whilst not untouched by Gothic influence, Duccio fundamentally owes most to the Byzantine exemplars. Unlike Giotto, he is not deeply concerned with the rendering of three-dimensional space, but his wonderful sense of colour and his melodious, effective silhouetting are consistently borne witness to by his production, of which it is characteristic that it should include no frescoes at all, but be restricted to panel pictures, glowing and glistening in tone. Among his many followers, Simone Martini† (1284 ?–1344) had great individual gifts; and, like Giotto, he carried the message of his art to different parts of the Italian peninsula. He died at Avignon in Southern France, the city of the exiled Popes, which was also visited, according to one early informant, by Giotto.

In the first half of the Trecento the influence of Siena began for that matter to make itself felt in the Florentine school: most of the masters who have been mentioned above, such as Bernardo Daddi, Andrea Bonaiuti and Agnolo Gaddi, may be quoted as exemplifying that influence. A channel through which the example of the art of Siena reached the Florentine school was the work of one of its most notable masters, Ambrogio Lorenzetti, who lived in Florence between 1332 and 1334, and whose brother, Pietro Lorenzetti (c. 1280–c. 1348), also was a painter of great distinction. Both, while remaining faithful to much of the native Sienese tradition, were noticeably affected by the example of Giotto's interpretation of form and sense of drama. Ambrogio Lorenzetti is especially remembered for his frescoes in the Palazzo Pubblico at Siena, symbolising Good and Bad Government in a series of elaborate compositions. It is easy to point out absurdities and exaggerations in these vast allegories, but they are nevertheless most impressive, both as a whole and in the details; and the manner in which the pursuits of the countryside, as well as life in the cities, are interpreted in them strikes a new and thrilling note. In many ways, affinities with them are present in the immense allegorical fresco known as *The Triumph of Death*, which is seen in the Campo Santo at Pisa, and conveys a terrifying impression of the Italy that was ravaged by the Black Death. This is, however, not by one of the Lorenzettis, but probably by a local Pisan master (Francesco Traini ?).

Local schools become recognisable almost throughout Italy during the Trecento. Two masters hailing from Verona, Altichiero and Avanzo, are responsible for various frescoes notably in Padua, which bear witness to a highly developed sense of colour, true power of incisive design and considerable gift for registering and interpreting the details of passing life. Belonging as they do to the end of the Trecento, they furnish a prelude to the work of another Veronese painter, Antonio Pisano,† called Pisanello (c. 1395–c. 1455)—also a famous medallist, who travelled widely in Italy, where he became one of the chief exponents of a very significant movement in late Gothic painting. Other prominent representatives of this movement were Don Lorenzo Monaco (c. 1370–c. 1425), a monk of the Order of the Camaldolese, who was born in Siena but went to live in Florence while still young, and Gentile da Fabriano (c. 1390–1427), a native of Umbria who, like Pisanello, in the course of a brilliant career, worked all over the peninsula.

The tendencies which these artists represent had an international diffusion in Europe at the time, as witness above all the illuminations of the magnificent *Book of Hours* of the Duc de Berry, painted by Pol de Limbourg and his brothers about 1410. The result is that these works produced north and south of the Alps have a curious family air. There undoubtedly is in them a sensitive realism of sorts—in some individual figures, in the rendering of animals, plants and flowers—but the structure of the human body is often entirely subordinated to an idea of rhythmic design expressed also in the sweeping late Gothic draperies; and with perspective the greatest liberties are taken. For all that, the result, from the imaginative point of view, is sometimes extraordinarily impressive, as, for instance, in Italy some compositions by Don Lorenzo Monaco prove most emphatically. Pictorial design in these works had quite spontaneously come curiously near to the methods which we know from the Far East. But a tremendous reaction was at hand.

CHAPTER III

IN Italian sculpture the reaction is associated with the name of Donatello (1386-1466), the Florentine ; and Florence it was that ushered in the phase which in art history is called the "Renaissance." We must beware, however, of exaggerating that aspect of the phase which stands for a "re-birth" of classical art—an aspect of which unduly much has formerly been made. In architecture it is true that the conventions of Gothic art are largely given up in Florence at the beginning of the *Quattrocento*, and much of the terminology of classical art is again adopted ; but the result bears a very superficial resemblance to classical architecture. As regards sculpture and painting, classical sculpture acquires a considerable value in supplying exemplars ; but no attempt is made to create a neo-classicism, for example of the kind which the late eighteenth century favoured.

The first "Renaissance" architect is Filippo Brunellesco (1377-1446). Like so many of the Italian characters of this period, he was a man of amazing universality of mind and ceaseless intellectual curiosity, and his ties of friendship with several artists made him a power of great and widespread influence. He was a pioneer in the scientific exploration of perspective, and at the beginning of his career he seriously considered taking up sculpture, in which he attained considerable proficiency. So much was this the case that when, in the year 1400, a competition took place among the sculptors of Italy for the task of decorating a pair of bronze doors for the Florence Baptistry with bas-reliefs, Brunellesco submitted a trial piece (which still survives) ; and the jury hesitated a long time between his work and that of the sculptor Lorenzo Ghiberti (1378-1455) before giving the order to the latter. Ghiberti

eventually became a figure of considerable importance in the Florentine school : his is not a formidable genius, after the fashion of Donatello, but his art breathes a sense of singular graceful beauty, with not a little of the Gothic manner still clinging to it ; and his command of the technical side of his art reaches perfection. With him there were apprenticed many young artists who eventually became famous as painters ; so that in Ghiberti the interconnection between Florentine painting and sculpture is strikingly illustrated.

Donatello is, however, the artist who truly holds a key position in the history of Quattrocento art ; for, famous though his influence on sculpture was, this is by no means the whole story—his achievement was of paramount importance for painting as well. Realism and the typically Italian dramatic power are the essentials of his art. A most vivid sense of structure is present in him—there is no question of his forms being made the vehicle purely of abstract harmonies of line, as the late Gothic artists tended to make them.

Donatello's long career falls quite naturally into three periods. The first period, which extends to about 1423, is marked by a series of large marble statues wrought for the Cathedral of Florence and for the front of the church in Florence known as the Or San Michele. He has found himself completely in his statue of *St. George* for the latter church ; the pose of the young knight, so firmly planted on his feet, the lines of the shield accentuating the simplicity of the disposition, mark the most decided contrast to the rhythmical devices no less of Gothic than of classical statuary.

The fame of Donatello was not long in growing, and, in order to cope with the numerous commissions received by him, he was obliged to rely on the help of pupils and assistants. Besides, having had several works in bronze ordered from him, and being himself unfamiliar with the technique of bronze casting, he entered into a kind of partnership with an expert at that technique, the sculptor Michelozzo; and the works executed in conjunction with the latter belong to the second phase of Donatello's activity, covering the years 1423–1444.

As the third and last period of Donatello's career we may regard that between 1444 and 1466, the year of his death. Nearly half this time was spent by Donatello away from Florence, he having in 1444 gone to Padua and stayed in that city without interruption until 1454. In Padua he produced the great equestrian monument of Gattamelata, the Commander-in-Chief of the armies of Venice, a work of marvellous harmony of proportion and deep psychological insight. Donatello's other great work in Padua was the decoration of the high altar for the church of St. Anthony, for which he produced a large number of bronze statues and bas-reliefs of populous scenes representing various miracles of St. Anthony, compositions of tremendous dramatic power, of which a distinct echo is traceable in several of Raphael's great frescoes in the Vatican, where he was faced with a kindred problem.

When Donatello died in 1466 he left Florentine sculpture completely transformed. As mentioned before, Florentine painting felt the effect of his art very strongly too; while in addition to this, his long residence at Padua made him a very important factor in the evolution of North Italian art, painting as well as sculpture.

Within the Florentine school of painting Masaccio † (1401–1428/29) occupies much the same position as Donatello does with regard to sculpture, very much briefer though his life was, and incomparably smaller though the number of the works produced by him is. It has already been stressed that his art

denotes the most tremendous contrast to the tendencies of late Gothic painting, which had reached such a wide diffusion at the beginning of the fifteenth century; and that in his dramatic expressiveness and in his interpretation of three-dimensional space he marks a return to the attitude of Giotto, whose tendencies he develops in accordance with the impulses of his own genius. One step beyond Giotto—at any rate as we know him with full certainty, and leaving conjectural possibilities out of account—is marked by Masaccio's deeply significant adoption of the device of *chiaroscuro*: the treatment of light and shade so as to articulate his compositions, keeping certain parts of them back and accentuating others.

Realism and solidity of structure Masaccio learnt without doubt largely from his friend Donatello; while his knowledge of perspective he owes in considerable measure to another older friend, Brunellesco. Thus this trio—Brunellesco, Donatello and Masaccio—stand quite incontestably at the head of Quattrocento art.

One further point of interest must be noted about Masaccio—although his art is in such striking contrast to the work of the late Gothic painters, there is nothing to suggest that he met with any of the embittered opposition that has been experienced by painters—Caravaggio, for instance, in the late sixteenth century, not to speak of the various great French masters in the nineteenth century.

Masaccio's message is really contained in the series of frescoes by him which survives in a small chapel—the Brancacci—in the Church of Santa Maria del Carmine at Florence; and the date of this fresco may be placed between 1422 and the time of Masaccio's death—1428/29. To some extent the questions affecting the frescoes in the Brancacci Chapel are complicated by the fact that the painter Masolino (1383–1447), Masaccio's alleged master at a fairly early date, is indicated as the author of some of these paintings; but the main thing is that the authorship of the principal frescoes—embodying the great reform in painting—is not in doubt as being Masaccio's. The frescoes in question are the *Expulsion from Paradise*,† unsurpassed in its dramatic power and its imaginative use of *chiaroscuro*; the *Tribute Money*, in which the story is set out in terms which, if simple, are of the most majestic pondus; *SS. Peter and John curing the Infirm with their Shadows*, deeply interesting as a new departure in composition, inasmuch as the principal figures move towards the spectator, as they never do in Giotto; and *St. Peter Baptising*, containing two extraordinarily fine studies of the nude.

Only a few panel pictures by Masaccio have come down to us; much the most important is his *Madonna and Child Enthroned between Angels making Music*, in the National Gallery, originally the main panel of an altarpiece on which Masaccio was working in 1426. The picture is remarkable for the wonderful beauty of its colouring—for to all his other gifts Masaccio also added that of a colourist of the highest order—and for the deep imaginative sympathy in the interpretation of the characters, which, as has been truly remarked, is curiously akin to that of Rembrandt.

It should be stressed once again that in spite of the small number of works left by Masaccio and the short space of years covered by his life, his influence on the history of painting is a decisive one, really creating "a new age"; and that influence was chiefly wielded by the frescoes in the Brancacci Chapel, which successive generations of young artists were busy incessantly copying.

Alongside of Masaccio, one of the chief masters working for the establishment of the new style in the Florentine school was an older contemporary of his, who also reached a much greater age, Fra Angelico ‡ (1387–1455). He joined the Dominican Order when he was twenty; the whole of his life was spent in an ecclesiastical atmosphere,

† Plate 11

into which atmosphere the mood of his works also carries us; but it would be a mistake to let these circumstances obscure the fact that Fra Angelico contributed powerfully towards making Masaccio's reform a success in the Florentine school. In the works which Fra Angelico carried out during his stay (1436–1447) in the Monastery of San Marco in Florence—perhaps the most significant phase of his career—his adherence to Masaccio's standard of structural draughtsmanship and conception of three-dimensional space is patent indeed; but the gentleness and meditative tenderness of the frescoes with which he decorated room after room stand in vivid contrast to Masaccio's thoughtful brusqueness of spirit. Apart from Florence, Fra Angelico worked in other places of Tuscany and Central Italy; and certain of his late frescoes in the Vatican have a strength and monumental quality which mark the consummation of his assimilation of Quattrocento ideals.

Fra Angelico also painted a great many panel pictures—always, of course, of sacred subjects—which are of singular lovableness, and in which forms and movements of the utmost gracefulness combine with colours of unsurpassed clearness and purity on a lustrous gold ground, to produce a deep and intensely characteristic impression. There are, too, in these works a wonderfully vivid and infectious delight in the settings of nature, in far-reaching vistas of mountains, in rhythmic succession of trees in full leaf and shining with golden fruit, and above all a delight in flowering lawns which Fra Angelico knew how to interpret with marvellous insight and sense of poetry.

The story of the successive generations of Quattrocento painters in Florence is one of never-flagging interest, and exhibits developments and experiments of far-reaching importance. Among the contemporaries of Masaccio, three notable masters must be singled out for mention, as exemplifying tendencies closely akin to those of the founder of the

‡ Plate 10

new style: Paolo Uccello, Andrea del Castagno and Domenico Veneziano. Paolo Uccello † (1397 ?–1475) was an enthusiast for the new science of perspective, which he explored with truly romantic fervour; but the study of perspective by no means summed up his significance as an artist. His three famous battle scenes, of which the National Gallery possesses one, *The Rout of San Romano*,† are superb compositions, full of the glamour of the last days of chivalry, and gorgeous in colour. A work in which his feeling for nature comes to the fore in truly fascinating a manner is his *Hunt by Moonlight*, in the Ashmolean Museum at Oxford, in which the scene is laid among the far-reaching colonnades of a wood, whose oak-trees are just turning brown with the arrival of autumn, and where the countless little figures of the members of the hunt, mounted and on foot, and the hounds stand out in clear limpid colours against a mysterious background of dusk as they dart forward in pursuit of the deer.

Andrea del Castagno ‡ (1410–1457) is an artist of a much more coarse and brutal fibre, but he has an undeniable force and power of monumental design, expressed in a style of statuesque figure-painting visibly affected by Donatello. One of his great works is the imposing fresco of *The Last Supper*,‡ which he painted for the refectory of the Monastery of Sant' Apollonia in Florence. The scene is here laid in a Roman banqueting hall, sumptuously decorated with variegated marbles. The figures of Apostles which people the room are conceived in a titanic spirit, disposed with the utmost simplicity yet without the slightest suggestion of primitive stiffness; and the whole is instinct with a spirit of monumental grandeur which nothing could surpass. Andrea del Castagno's interest in the problems of perspective is thoroughly characteristic of the governing tendencies of the period to which he belongs. In many ways much akin to him, though by no means as brutal a realist,

is Domenico Veneziano (*c.* 1450–1461), much of whose work has unfortunately perished; there survives, however, a great altar-piece by him, the principal panel of which, *The Madonna and Saints*, is now in the Uffizi in Florence; while the panels of the predella, scattered all over the world, have of recent years been identified: two of them are at the Fitzwilliam Museum at Cambridge, and evince both originality and power.

A contemporary of the artists just mentioned, yet marking a very great contrast to them, was one of the most notable figures in the history of the Florentine school— Fra Filippo Lippi † (1406 ?–1469). With him we find none of the interests in the serious and scholarly problems of art which originated with Masaccio—on the contrary, he may be described as essentially the descendant of the late Gothic painters. But his art has an extraordinary charm, being expressive of a graceful, roguish spirit which is essentially Fra Filippo's own. He is one of the very greatest masters of colour whom Florence ever produced. His Bohemian habits, friar though he was, got him into countless difficulties and complications, out of which he was very patiently helped by the Medici family, the rulers of Florence. Important frescoes exist by him at Prato and Spoleto, though not at Florence; the works by him of which one instinctively thinks in the first instance are, however, his panel pictures, notably those in which the scene is laid in the Florentine palaces with their cool, diffused light—see, for instance, his *Madonna and Child*, in the Palazzo Pitti at Florence, or his renderings of the Holy Family in rocky, woodland solitudes.

From these Florentine masters we may now turn to those somewhat younger members of the school who came to the fore mainly about the middle of the Quattrocento. And here we must first notice the painter Alesso Baldovinetti ‡ (1425–1499), who is recorded as Domenico Veneziano's assistant, as is also the great Umbrian master Piero

† Plate 9   ‡ Plate 18   † Plate 12   ‡ Plate 15

MARS AND VENUS *by Sandro Botticelli* (1444-1510)

Plate 2

Wood $27\frac{1}{2}'' \times 68''$

ella Francesca, of whom more will be said ter. Baldovinetti did much towards the onquest of landscape by art—does not asari in a famous passage hold up as notable is portrayal of "rivers, bridges, stones, erbs, fruit, woods, fields, castles, squares and ther similar things"?—and his Madonnas ave a strange flower-like beauty as well s a wonderful sense of monumental quality. nother contemporary Florentine master as Antonio del Pollaiuolo † (1433–1498), also nown as a distinguished sculptor. He was uch interested in the study of the nude— e is said to have been one of the first artists o practise dissection of human bodies. His nterpretation of intense muscular tension in he nude human figure is not only masterly n itself but set an important example for hose who followed after him.

Another painter-sculptor of importance vas Andrea del Verrocchio (1435–1488),

the master of Leonardo da Vinci; his crowning achievement is not a painting, but the equestrian monument of the Venetian General Colleoni at Venice, of tremendous dramatic power, even if on a lower imaginative plane than Donatello's *Gattamelata*. Nor must we pass over Fra Filippo Lippi's pupil, Francesco Pesellino (1422–1457), whose short life gave more than a brilliant promise to some extent along the lines struck out by his master, but yet with an individuality definitely his own. A pupil of Fra Angelico's was Benozzo Gozzoli (1420–1497), who worked with tremendous ease, and who at times becomes a somewhat prolix, not to say trivial, narrator, but who also produced works of very real charm. He worked in many places, but has left one of his best works in Florence, his fresco of the *Journey of the Magi* continuously set out on the walls of the Palazzo Riccardi.

CHAPTER IV

OF the masters who achieved prominence in the Florentine school of the second half of the fifteenth century, Sandro Botticelli ‡ (1444–1510) now claims attention. It is a notable fact that a well-informed contemporary judge (c. 1485) should stress the "virile air" (*aria virile*) among his characteristics; we are apt to think in the first instance of the highly strung sensitiveness which marks his art. He was the pupil of Fra Filippo Lippi; and the link of affinity with the latter artist is undoubtedly there temperamentally in the feeling of lyrical poetry which pervades the work of Botticelli; but it is poetry of a very different kind from that of the gay and irresponsible Fra Filippo. On the other hand, Botticelli's style of figure drawing owes not a little to that of Pollaiuolo and also to that of Verrocchio.

Works such as the *Primavera* and *The Birth of Venus* (both in the Uffizi Gallery,

Florence), which he painted for one of the Medici, have intense charm of romantic sentiment, expressed in a language of art which in no wise savours of neo-classicism, but which derives its power both from Botticelli's exquisite melodious line and his perfect command of facial expression. Late in life, Botticelli came under the influence of the revivalist propaganda of Savonarola, the reformer-monk; and the effect is seen in several of his pictures (such as the *Nativity* in the National Gallery) in which the sentiment tends to reach the pitch of hysteria.

If poetry is the keynote of Botticelli's art, prose is that of the work of Domenico Ghirlandaio † (1449–1494), the great fresco painter who is said to have expressed the wish that he might be given the circuit of the city walls of Florence to decorate. A pupil of Alesso Baldovinetti, Ghirlandaio chiefly worked in Florence, though various

† Plate 22 ‡ Colour Plate 2, Plate 25

† Plate 19

frescoes serve to prove his activities also elsewhere, notably in Rome, where several Florentine painters (including Botticelli) worked in the Sistine Chapel. There exist relatively few panel pictures by him. The work in which his career culminates is the decoration of the choir of the Church of Santa Maria Novella at Florence, an imposing series of frescoes of the life of St. John the Baptist † and the life of the Virgin—paintings completed in 1490, when, as a contemporary inscription records, "the most beautiful city ennobled by riches, victories, arts and buildings was in full enjoyment of prosperity, health and peace." As a record of the life of Florence at the time nothing could surpass these frescoes in completeness and accuracy; and the outward characteristics of the Florentine population to this day—and, for that matter, of the peasants in the Tuscan country all around—are indeed portrayed in the works of Ghirlandaio with real power, hard and jerky though his art undoubtedly is, and without any sense of the dramatic. Notably, the way in which dense rows of portrait figures tend to crowd his compositions as spectators is symptomatic of his whole artistic outlook.

A slightly younger contemporary of Botticelli's and Ghirlandaio's was Filippino Lippi ‡ (1457–1504). He was only twelve when his father died, so he is not likely to have learnt very much from him; his really important years of study, though he was young enough even then, were spent under Botticelli—himself, it will be remembered, Fra Filippo's pupil. Great precocity was quite clearly a characteristic of Filippino's: his finest effort in many ways is his *Virgin Appearing to St. Bernard*,‡ in the Church of the Badia in Florence, which the young master finished in 1482. Yet even here the art of Filippino is somewhat verging on the commonplace—he cannot help playing to the gallery. Shortly afterwards Filippino was entrusted with a task which must have struck a Florentine master of the Quattrocento as honourable

above all others—to complete the decoration of the Brancacci Chapel, which had not been fully carried out by Masaccio. Filippino evidently felt it incumbent upon him to do his very best; and it is very interesting to see how he endeavoured to approximate to Masaccio's style as far as it was in him. As a result, though the mannerisms of Filippino are patent enough, the whole is undoubtedly one of the most satisfactory efforts of the artist. Later in life, Filippino tended to cultivate the bizarre and to become restless and exaggerated. His development in this direction is seen clearly in his fresco of the Assumption of the Virgin, which forms part of a series painted for the Church of Santa Maria sopra Minerva in Rome.

A Florentine master of considerable interest, belonging to the end of the Quattrocento, is Piero di Cosimo † (1462–1521). What we know of his life shows him to have been the most eccentric of men; and his art, too, reflects a very whimsical and extravagant fancy, coupled, however, with an extraordinary delicacy and childlike gracefulness of sentiment. The works in which the individual tendencies of Piero di Cosimo find their most clear and charming expression are his scenes from pagan mythology; and among them the most perfect is his *Death of Procris*,† in the National Gallery—a work of which it is no exaggeration to say that the qualities both of design and expression entitle it to rank among the finest productions of Italian art. A point of technique is notable with Piero di Cosimo; he was eventually able to master a method of oil painting. The traditional technique in the Italian school was tempera, by which the colours were tempered by yolk of egg. Various experiments in technique had been carried out by successive generations of Florentine fifteenth-century painters; among those in that school whose works show an oil technique, Piero di Cosimo is one of the earliest.

Among the schools of Tuscany, that of Siena, which had such noble traditions, continued a most prolific one all through the Quattrocento; but a great change had taken place in the part played by Siena in the general evolution of Italian painting. We have seen how in the Trecento the Sienese' school wielded a decisive influence, for instance on the Florentine school; in the Quattrocento that influence practically ceases to exist. Pictorially, Siena now almost recedes within her own district. Still, work of immense charm continued to be produced in Siena: as witness among late Gothic painters Sassetta (1392–1450), whose interpretation of the Franciscan legend in the National Gallery entitles him to a true place of honour, and Giovanni di Paolo (1403–1482). Subsequent Quattrocento painters of distinction in Siena, reflecting the changed conditions of the times, are Francesco di Giorgio, immensely gifted sculptor as well as painter; and Matteo di Giovanni (c. 1435–1495), in whom the true Sienese note of decorative effectiveness survives to the last, but who also has a remarkable grasp of form and power of dramatic effect.

In Umbria the great and imposing figure of Piero della Francesca † (1416 ?–1498) rises above all other masters of the Quattrocento: his art marks, indeed, one of the supreme achievements of Italian painting. He owes something to Florence, for early in life he worked there as Domenico Veneziano's assistant; afterwards, while never breaking the ties which bound him to his native Borgo San Sepolcro among the Apennines, his art took him in a triumphal progress to many Italian cities. Monumental quality stamps his art in the most impressive fashion, and he has a truly consummate feeling for design, which with him is built upon entirely personal, staid and majestic rhythms, favouring forms of great massiveness; and equally his sense of colour and atmosphere is as individual as it is exquisite. Only one fairly complete cycle of frescoes by him now survives, *The Story of the True Cross* in the Church of San Francesco at Arezzo, painted

probably about 1455–1460. Never was there a more impressive picture-chronicle, across the centuries, with the imaginative standard always remaining on the same sublime plane. Single frescoes by him remain in different places, and among them the tremendous *Resurrection* † in the Town Hall at Borgo San Sepolcro must be singled out for mention as one of the master's key conceptions. The surviving panel pictures by Piero della Francesca are rare, and the National Gallery is fortunate in possessing two of the most important, *The Baptism of Christ* and *The Nativity*. The peculiar greatness of the artist speaks from them in no uncertain terms: technically they denote his development from the tempera technique to a method of oil painting, reminiscent of the Flemish school.

Piero della Francesca had three great pupils, Melozzo da Forli, Luca Signorelli and Pietro Perugino. Whatever they assimilated from him, they also possessed such marked personalities of their own that there is no question of any of them suggesting the derivation from Piero della Francesca.

Of the production of Melozzo da Forli ‡ (1438–1494) very little has come down to us, but enough survives to show that Piero's restraint and crushing relentlessness are replaced in Melozzo by a warm pulsation of life and exuberance of action; yet a true monumental quality is always present in the latter. Especially memorable among Melozzo's works are the fragments of his great *Ascension* ‡ from the apse of the Church of SS. Apostoli, a composition carried out consistently in a perspective dictated by the view from below and reaching an entrancing lyrical beauty in the figures of angels playing on musical instruments.

Judging from the style of his works, Luca Signorelli (c. 1450–1523) must have followed the example of his own first master, Piero della Francesca, in making direct contact with the Florentine school: his drawing of the nude and rendering of effects of vigorous muscular movement point quite clearly to an acquaintance with the art of Pollaiulo. Signorelli is essentially an artist of titanic force and overwhelming dramatic power : he has none of Piero's Olympic restraint nor his interest in atmospheric effects ; and conceptions of such entrancing loveliness as Melozzo's angels are altogether foreign to him. The most impressive manifestation of Signorelli's genius are his frescoes in the Cappella di San Brizio in Orvieto Cathedral ; here he has set out the closing scenes of the Christian epic of the world in a series of vast compositions which show the true range and individual bent of his imagination, and contain many definite anticipations of Michelangelo's art. Signorelli was born at Cortona in Northern Umbria and spent most of his life there surrounded by the regard of his fellow-citizens, much as Piero della Francesca did at Borgo San Sepolcro.

Pietro Perugino † (c.1446–1523), the third of the pupils of Piero della Francesca mentioned, is an artist of very real significance, who at the beginning of his career experienced a succession of influences—including that of Verrocchio in Florence and of Signorelli nearer home—but eventually developed a style very markedly his own. His heart goes out to compositions of lovely, spacious quality in which the melodious character of his line is harmoniously matched ; and settled in the hill city of Perugia, " Pietro of Perugia " interprets in the happiest fashion the softness of tints and the delicacy of silhouettes of the Umbrian countryside. He was able gradually to master an oil technique of great accomplishment, which in his panel pictures aided him greatly towards achieving his aims as a landscape painter. At his best and most characteristic, his work breathes an exquisite, tender and contemplative atmosphere without any note of drama stressed. He is, however, apt to repeat himself and to fall into banality and over-sweetness, yet when all is said and done his achievement is of tremendous significance.

Producing with great ease (and not only in Umbria), he also inspired a host of followers ; one of the most notable of the earlier ones is Bernardino Pinturicchio (c. 1454–1514), in many ways decidedly provincial, yet in certain of his works—notably the glorious frescoes in the Cathedral library at Siena— of a truly exhilarating character. It is, however, because some of the characteristics of Perugino descended upon, and were further developed by, Raphael that such an importance attaches to Perugino as a factor in the history of art.

CHAPTER V

WE may now turn to a consideration of the school of painting of Venice, which was to rival in importance the Florentine school of painting. It is not going too far if we claim that the sun and colour of the city of the lagoons in themselves stimulated the peculiar idiosyncrasies of the Venetian painters ; the contact between Venice and Byzantium and the splendour-loving East generally was a close one already at an early period, and affected the artistic destinies of Venice powerfully. The incomparable Byzantine mosaics of St. Mark's were carried out in the main between the eleventh and the thirteenth centuries. In the course of the Trecento the absolute predominance of the Byzantine style begins to give way and the principles of style of Gothic art gradually penetrate into Venice. Composite altarpieces, with richly carved frames, formed the principal output of the Venetian painters during the Trecento ; but in the course of the century a most imposing series of narrative frescoes was begun in the hall of the

Plate 3

VIRGIN AND CHILD by *Filippino Lippi* (1457-1504)

Original 33½″ diameter

Grand Council in the Doges' Palace, and this points the way to that style of pageantry in painting which was to be so much cultivated in Venice.

Towards the end of that century was born Jacopo Bellini (c. 1395–1470), of whose pictures but a few have come down to us; his two sketch-books, however, in the British Museum and the Louvre, give an idea of the extraordinary range of his art, which was one that essentially found its scope in the Scriptural subjects in the Assembly Halls of the Scuolas, or great religious mutual aid societies of Venice; and in many ways the work of this late Gothic artist—a pupil of Gentile da Fabriano's—anticipates the subsequent development of the Venetian school.

About the middle of the Quattrocento, Padua, the old university town not far from Venice, became for a while the most important centre of influence in North Italian painting. This was ultimately due to the work of one man, Francesco Squarcione (1397–c. 1470), who had a tremendous talent as an organiser and who had hit upon a notion of classicism which in many ways was romantically misconstrued, but which did affect a great many artists of those parts. The greatest of them all was Andrea Mantegna † (c. 1431–1506), who was an enthusiast about all that savoured of classical sculpture and went in for rigid definition of form and plastic relief; but there is, too, in him a note of vehement passion which makes him a next-of-kin of Donatello's—little wonder that the example of Donatello, so long settled in Padua, should have affected him a great deal. A numerous following sprang up round these two masters, and many local schools scattered across North Italy go to make up a fascinating picture of great richness and complexity. Perhaps the principal of these local schools is that of Ferrara, tending to be strikingly unhackneyed in composition, not to speak of the remarkable sense of colour which characterises these Ferrarese artists, of whom Cosimo Tura ‡ (1420 ?–1496), Francesco del Cossa (1435 ?–

1477) and Ercole de Roberti (1450 ?–1496) are the most important.

Mantegna and the Bellini family were linked together by ties of relationship when in 1453 Mantegna married Jacopo Bellini's daughter Niccolosia; and the influence of Mantegna was strongly felt by the two sons of Jacopo, Gentile and Giovanni Bellini, both of whom became very distinguished artists, Giovanni, indeed, ending by being the head of the Venetian school of his time.

Gentile Bellini † (1429 ?–1507) above all went in for stately, ceremonial subjects which offered opportunities for depicting the pageants and processions which peopled the squares and canals of Venice; he shows great power as a portrait-painter and an exquisite sense of atmosphere, while his compositions have true monumental quality.

The work of Giovanni Bellini‡ (c. 1430–1516) covers a period of more than half a century from about 1460 to his death, and there can be little doubt that, in any case, soon after 1480 he was looked upon by general consent as the central figure of the Venetian school. His career presents the spectacle of a singularly long process of development by which Giovanni Bellini worked his way towards the principles of style which were to predominate in the Venetian school during its period of full maturity in the Cinquecento. Richness and harmony of colour are present already in Bellini's earliest works, and so is his striving after effects of atmospheric envelopment, in which he continued, with ever-increasing success, right to the end of his career. He was helped in his endeavour by the technical reform associated with the name of the painter Antonello da Messina (c. 1430–1479), who in 1475–1476 brought to Venice the Flemish oil technique of the Van Eycks, with which he had probably become acquainted through Jan Van Eyck's pupil, Petrus Cristus at Milan. At the outset we also find with Giovanni Bellini a complete realisation of the idea of mood in landscape and of its

† Plate 20   ‡ Plate 14   † Plate 16   ‡ Plate 17

value in heightening the imaginative effects of the compositions. The extreme intensity of religious feeling and tragic mood which characterise his earlier works gradually give way to a feeling of more purely delightful sensuousness and charm; but the lyrical and romantic note never disappears from his conceptions. In his rendering of form we find how he advances towards greater amplitude; also, the flow of his line gets by and by more easy, and his massing of light and shade broader and more effective.

The subject of the Madonna and Child was the central one in Giovanni Bellini's work, whether it took the form of the simple group for family devotion or the more elaborate compositions of the altar-pieces with saints. Early in his career he painted some marvellous pictures of the Passion of Christ, notably the *Pietà*; and he was also a portrait-painter of much sympathy and insight.

The painters of Venice who belong to the following of Giovanni Bellini form a very numerous group: among those who still rank as Quattrocento masters, we may here mention the noble and scholarly Cima da Conegliano (*c.* 1460–1517/18), singularly responsive to the appeal of landscape, and Vittore Carpaccio (*c.* 1460–*c.* 1525), spontaneous and entertaining at all times. The great artist who issued from the atelier of Giovanni Bellini, and with whom a new chapter in the history of art begins, is Giorgione† (*c.* 1477–1510); and here something must be said about the different conditions which witnessed the establishment of the Cinquecento style in Venice and in Florence.

It cannot be sufficiently stressed that when the style of the Cinquecento is reached in Venice, nothing in the nature of something essentially revolutionary takes place. As we have seen, Giovanni Bellini's aims as an artist lie in the same direction as those of Giorgione, although undoubtedly Giorgione's own power of individual creation and his intensity of youthful conviction give an altogether new life to his earliest efforts. This continuity of effort in succeeding generations of artists, leading to the establishment of the sixteenth-century style in Venice, stands in significant contrast to the conditions which governed the corresponding phase of artistic evolution in Florence. Florence is characteristically apt to proceed by revolution. In the Florentine school a new style—the style of Leonardo, Michelangelo and Fra Bartolomeo—meant to a great extent a violent reaction against the tendencies which had become current in the latter part of the Quattrocento—a break with the tradition of a Botticelli, a Filippino Lippi and a Ghirlandaio, and the return to the great dramatic and monumental traditions of a Masaccio, and, harking back from him, of a Giotto.

Giorgione was born at Castelfranco, a small city charmingly situated on the Venetian mainland in a rich wooded plain at the foot of the Alps; and in the landscape backgrounds of his pictures we have no difficulty in recognising the picturesque motifs of the country of his birth. His rise to fame in Venice was meteoric, but his career came tragically to an end when he died of the plague in 1510. Unfortunately for posterity, a considerable proportion of his life's work was of necessity doomed to have a very ephemeral existence—the frescoes with which he adorned the fronts of a number of palaces in Venice. For other paintings his name has frequently been claimed in past years; but recent criticism has justly brought down the number of works that may be assigned to him to a very small figure—a little more than a dozen. In all these, however, is revealed an artistic genius of supreme greatness, and even if his life's work had been restricted just to them—which we know it was not—we should have little difficulty in understanding the tremendous influence wielded by him; for think what the example of Masaccio meant to the Florentine school and how much as regards mere numbers

† Plates 30 and 31

is achievement fell short even of that of Giorgione !

At the head of Giorgione's work stands his great altar-piece in his native city, the *Madonna and Child Enthroned with Two Saints*.† The formality of the arrangement here surpasses anything in Giovanni Bellini, of whom many details remind us ; but the whole is conceived as a romantic, chivalrous homage to the Madonna, and that is quite distinctly Giorgione's way. In the absence of any ornament in the Madonna's dress, in the increased feeling for structure which prompts the unveiling of her neck, we see characteristic signs of the Cinquecento ; and in the very choice of the colours one also feels the presence of a young genius with his strongly individual note.

The intimate harmony between figures and landscape here is, of course, entirely in the tradition of Giovanni Bellini. The subject of the picture presents no obscurity ; but there are other works in which the details of the literary invention are far from easy to unravel—as, for instance, in the famous picture called *Giorgione's Family*,‡ now in the Venice Gallery—and it is not sure that this is only due to the inadequacy of Giorgione's present-day interpreters. We must remember that when Vasari visited Venice only some thirty years after the death of Giorgione, he could find no one to explain to him the subjects on the front of one of the Palaces painted by Giorgione ; and Vasari expresses the opinion that in designing those compositions Giorgione had entirely given himself up to his fancy. The earliest description of *Giorgione's Family*, due to a highly civilised contemporary of Giorgione's, runs simply : " The landscape with the storm, the gipsy woman and the child." But even if there is some literary invention at the bottom of it all, Giorgione has obviously not concerned himself with the telling of a definite story : he has aimed at conveying an intensely romantic glamorous mood, and in that endeavour he has certainly been

† Plate 30

supremely successful. In the composition we notice—as often in Giorgione—a tendency to build the design on a rectangular play of lines, but there is here a richness and freedom of rhythm which are absent in the earlier works. The picture also shows a marked advance towards greater breadth and freedom of handling.

A picture which Giorgione did not live to finish, and which was completed by Titian, is the famous *Venus Asleep* in the Dresden Gallery. It makes, indeed, a fitting close to his career, for here Giorgione has fully succeeded in realising that ideal of classical purity of form which haunts him towards the end of his life ; and as a whole this is also one of Giorgione's most consummately beautiful designs. In the sentiment of which the picture is expressive there is a strange suggestion of tragedy, which it is easier to feel than to account for.

The connection between Titian and Giorgione in this work is symbolical. Titian, who felt the influence of Giorgione so strongly, after the premature death of the latter rose to a position among the Venetian painters of his time corresponding to Giovanni Bellini's during an earlier period ; and his ultimate development then led him far indeed from his early Giorgionesque manner. Titian was probably by some years—not very many—the junior of Giorgione, and according to tradition studied, like Giorgione, under Giovanni Bellini ; but it is a remarkable fact that while the connection with Giovanni Bellini's style is very distinct in the early works of Giorgione, the early works of Titian do not remind us of Giovanni Bellini—except indirectly—but only of Giorgione. Giorgione thus comes to occupy an altogether central position in the history of Venetian painting : on the one hand still closely in touch with the Quattrocento tradition represented by Giovanni Bellini, and on the other hand pointing the way to the marvellous development of Titian and all that followed after him.

‡ Plate 31

CHAPTER VI

THE Cinquecento style in Florence, to which we now return, is a stirring phase of art, the representatives of which are legion, painters as well as sculptors; and something has been said above of the conditions under which that style came into being and the significance which attaches to the new movement. The first Cinquecento artist is Leonardo da Vinci (1452–1519), who, indeed, establishes the new clarified and monumental style in Florence even before the Quattrocento, as regards mere chronology, had run to its end. A good deal younger than him is Michelangelo Buonarroti (1475–1564), who yet by the side of Leonardo, at the beginning of the sixteenth century, impressively typifies one glorious moment in the history of Florentine art. With these two must be associated a third of comparable stature artistically, who, although not a Florentine but an Umbrian, also as regards his artistic orientation, yet profited enormously by his studies in Florence early in the Cinquecento, becoming perhaps the most harmonious and balanced personality in the whole domain of Italian art—Raphael (Raffaello Santi, 1483–1520). Treating of this trio will bring the present outline of Italian art to its close.

Of all the richly gifted characters of the Italian Renaissance, Leonardo was perhaps the most astounding. There was scarcely any field of human thought and research that Leonardo—devoured by an all-pervading intellectual curiosity and possessed of incomparable powers of observation and induction—did not explore with amazing success. All that, however, we are not concerned with here: in this connection he is primarily the supreme artist, whose range, for that matter, is truly amazing too. And on this point it is important to realise that the free and unfettered work of sketching and designing and experimenting was much more congenial to him than the laborious carrying out of a fixed project. He will make no end of sketches of a given subject, working out all sorts of alternatives and studying the most minute details; but the cases in which he actually began the painting on wall or panel are very few, and fewer still are those in which he carried to a finish the work that he had begun. Hence there is no artist for the knowledge of whom the study of his drawings assumes greater importance than precisely Leonardo: fortunately, drawings by him survive in considerable numbers.

Leonardo studied under Andrea del Verrocchio, in whose studio he remained for a fairly long time—at any rate up to 1476—and in 1481 he undertook to paint *The Adoration of the Magi*,† which still survives (in the Uffizi, Florence). Here the great reform has in all essentials been carried out. It is interesting to note that some points of resemblance to a picture of the same subject by Botticelli are definitely present; but the differences are also very great and significant. The whole design breathes a new spirit of monumental quality and simplification, which does not, however, by any means interfere with the expression of intense dramatic emotion. The number of figures is incomparably smaller, and the composition is built on much more severely architectural principles. The Madonna is again in the middle of the picture, not pushed towards one side; the central pyramid is clearly emphasised, there being no figures right in front of the Madonna—a very important feature this—and the whole is enclosed by tall, pillar-like figures at each end. The onset of the figures from the sides tells, in consequence, all the stronger.

† Plate 27

We see thus exemplified one of the main tendencies of natural Renaissance art—" to suggest much by little," grasping the essentials and not indulging in countless detailed statements, as the late Quattrocento in Florence is apt to do—the principles, in short, of Giotto and Masaccio.

Altogether foreign to Botticelli is also Leonardo's idea of *chiaroscuro*, with the light concentrated on the principal figures and the others enveloped in shadow; and here again we see how Leonardo takes up and further develops the tendencies of Masaccio. Also different from Botticelli's more purely subjective attitude is the interest which Leonardo shows in the intimate characterisation of the various actors in the drama. On this point he continues the traditions of his master Verrocchio; and in some of these heads we can already see that power of expressing the utmost gracefulness and charm in which Leonardo is perhaps unsurpassed.

Soon after commencing *The Adoration of the Magi*, Leonardo went to Milan, where he stayed at the Court of the ruler, Lodovico il Moro, for about sixteen years. Among the first pictures which he (1483) undertook to paint in Milan—" in oil "—was *The Virgin of the Rocks* † (Louvre), fascinating as a composition, as an interpretation of the characters and in its study of plants and flowers. The great and central production of Leonardo's Milanese period, and one of the crowning achievements of Renaissance art, carried out probably between 1495 and 1497, is the fresco of *The Last Supper* in the monastery of Santa Maria delle Grazie. The experiments in technique in which Leonardo indulged over this painting did not make for its durability; it has, moreover, been drastically repainted and gravely neglected (indeed, its saga almost came to the most tragic of conclusions in much-bombed Milan, but it seems that although the building was hit the fresco is much as before); and as it stood, *The Last Supper* enabled one to gain a

† Plate 29

definite idea of what it once was. The grasp of the dramatic situation was entirely in the tradition of Masaccio and Giotto; while the peculiar idiosyncrasies of Leonardo could be seen in the close study of varied psychology, as well as physiognomical subtleties.

Most lamentably barren of results were Leonardo's efforts centring round the equestrian monument of Francesco Sforza—father of Lodovico il Moro—which, with Donatello's *Gattamelata* and Verrocchio's *Colleoni*, was to have completed a trio of the utmost significance in the history of art. From numerous notes and sketches, we see the intense interest which Leonardo brought to his task; and he was finally able to prepare a huge clay model of the horse, which was acclaimed on all sides as a perfect marvel of art. That was not long before Lodovico il Moro's downfall in 1499, and the work never advanced any farther. Even the clay model soon perished, though we have no authentic confirmation of the story that after the French had captured Milan in 1499 it was used as a target by their archers. The sketches and models executed by Leonardo for this monument exercised, however, an enormous influence on later sculpture.

To the very end of Leonardo's Milanese period probably belongs the great cartoon of St. Anne, the Virgin, the Infant Christ and the Young Baptist, now at Burlington House: singularly grand in its conception and expressive of a mystery and haunting power peculiarly Leonardo's own. By 1500 Leonardo had returned to Florence and, except for an absence of about one year while he was serving Cesare Borgia as a military engineer, he continued to live at Florence till 1506. During this second Florentine period he carried out several important works. Among them two stand out—his portrait of *Mona Lisa* † and his cartoon of *The Battle of Anghiari*. The former is perhaps the most fascinatingly poetical of all Leonardo's works, as well as his most marvellous feat from the pictorial point of view; the latter unfortunately is

† Plate 28

known to us only from copies, which, however, with some drawings convey to us a distinct notion of the significance of the work. The cartoon was prepared for a fresco to be painted in the Great Hall of the Palazzo Vecchio at Florence, representing the battle between the Florentines and Milanese at Anghiari many years ago.

In the next year an order for a fresco of another scene from Florentine history, to be painted in the same locality, was given to Michelangelo. The two greatest living artists of Florence were thus made to work in direct and open rivalry. The cartoons for the two frescoes were duly finished, eliciting the greatest admiration; and just as before all artists had been wont to congregate at the Brancacci Chapel, to copy the frescoes of Masaccio, so they now flocked to the hall where the cartoons of Leonardo and Michelangelo were shown, to study and copy these. Leonardo even began to paint the fresco, but the work was never completed, and ultimately both cartoons perished. Leonardo's aim was clearly to convey as vivid a sensation as possible of the furious *mêlée* of the battle, of the blind passion animating the combatants—riders and horses alike; and how successful he was in achieving that end is evident from all the data.

From 1506 to 1513 Leonardo lived principally in Milan, and subsequently spent three years in Rome. Then, in 1516, he went to France at the invitation of Francis I; and it was in France that he died in 1519. Of his extant works, the latest in date are the pictures of *St. Anne, the Virgin and the Infant Christ* and *St. John the Baptist*, in the Louvre, which is the collection where Leonardo, that rarest of great painters, is most fully represented.

Michelangelo's life was a long one—close upon ninety years—and his work brings before us several aspects of artistic production—sculpture, painting, architecture. Sculpture was the form of art which was most congenial to him, and as an old man, looking back upon his life and with all sorts of great performances of other kinds to his credit, he felt genuinely sorry that he had not been able always to concentrate on sculpture. In 1488, as a boy of thirteen, he entered the workshop of Domenico Ghirlandaio; but he soon deserted painting for sculpture, which at the time formed the subject of special encouragement on the part of Lorenzo de' Medici. As things turned out, Michelangelo did paint a great deal, but this was fundamentally not due to any urge to do so; in one of his sonnets, which describes him painting the ceiling of the Sistine Chapel in Rome, he ends up bitterly: " This is not the right place for me : I am no painter."

We have noted the universality which is so essential a characteristic of Leonardo's outlook as an artist. With Michelangelo, things are different : the one and only object of study is the human figure, and principally the *nude* figure, out of which he extracts the most magnificent rhythmic harmonies of pose and movement. All through his art there runs the same feeling of heroic grandeur, and where he is most himself he makes his figures expressive of the overwhelming tragedy of existence, of the hopeless struggle of a noble and lofty mind with inexorable fate. He is one of the most purely subjective artists that have ever existed, tending to convert every subject that he attacks into a symbol of his own personal outlook on life.

After having laid the foundation of his fame through several of his early sculptures, Michelangelo, as we saw, in 1504 agreed to paint, in competition with Leonardo, a fresco for the Palazzo Vecchio in Florence. The painting itself was never even begun, but the cartoon (like Leonardo's, alas ! not surviving) was immensely admired. We can now only judge of it from insufficient reproductions, but it is evident that Michelangelo gave of his best in a scene of heroic muscular nudes in vigorous action—soldiers surprised by the enemy whilst bathing. Michelangelo discontinued the work, as Pope Julius II had asked him to undertake a great work of sculpture—the tomb of the Pope himself, to be set up in St. Peter's in Rome. Michelangelo took up the task with enthusiasm, but the Pope's interest in it soon flagged: he wanted Michelangelo to suspend his work on it and instead devote himself to the painting of the ceiling of the Sistine Chapel in the Vatican. It came to a violent conflict between these two formidable and ungovernable tempers: in the end Michelangelo had to give in, and between 1508 and 1512 he carried out the work which stands in the centre of his production and marks one of the culminations of Italian art: a sublime interpretation of scenes from Genesis, of Prophets and Sybils and various other subjects.† The tomb of Julius II was completed only much later and on a much reduced scale, for the Church of San Pietro in Vincoli in Rome: it incorporates, however, the magnificent statue of *Moses* which is one of Michelangelo's most striking works. Two wonderful statues of *Prisoners*, now in the Louvre, intended for the tomb, must be mentioned as giving the quintessence of Michelangelo's outlook on life expressed in the artistic form most natural to him.

To the 1520's belong the tombs of two Medici princes in San Lorenzo, Florence. Both these tombs are identically designed in a way which marks an entire break with the conventions of tomb sculpture. The figure of the deceased, recumbent in death, occurs nowhere: he is represented as a seated figure in a niche in the wall, and on the sarcophagus two recumbent allegorical figures have taken his place. No attempt is made by Michelangelo to reconstruct given historical characters in the figures of the dead princes; his sole concern is to make them expressive of emotional states.

As a fresco painter we again encounter Michelangelo in the Sistine Chapel, where between 1534 and 1541 he painted the gigantic composition of *The Last Judgment*—a formidable piece of pictorial rhetoric which

† Plates 32 and 33

left a most profound impress on Italian and indeed European art, and later still are the frescoes in the Cappella Paolina in the Vatican. They were finished when the master was over seventy, and show no sign of waning imaginative power. Soon after 1550 the aged master was no longer capable of the physical exertion connected with the work of a sculptor or a painter. He henceforth devoted himself entirely to architecture; from 1547 he had been superintending the rebuilding of St. Peter's, a work which continued to claim his attention until his death in 1564. No artist, it may be said in conclusion, has realised the Cinquecento ideal of grandeur more completely than Michelangelo, especially in sculpture.

The rise of Raphael † to fame was a rapid one, and the prestige achieved by him among his contemporaries was enormous; also, the brevity of his life added a vivid touch of drama to his career, thereby serving his posthumous fame. Yet Raphael has not had his best advocates among many of the enthusiasts that his art has called forth: too many have seen and praised in him above all the painter of sweet Madonnas. Indeed, great movements in modern art—such as realism and impressionism in nineteenth-century France—took definitely a derogatory view of him; and yet, the great and permanent qualities of his art are such that nothing can obscure them for long.

He is essentially a born designer, and as such he continues the tradition of spacious and melodious composition that had been evolved in his native Umbria by his master, Pietro Perugino. But having absorbed all that Perugino could give him, he felt the need of something beyond that: the structural draughtsmanship and the grasp of form which had developed in Florence; and by 1504 we find him in that city, which for that matter was frequently enough visited by Perugino. He learnt a great deal of essential importance from what he saw of the works of Leonardo and Michelangelo and many of

† Colour Plate 4, Plates 34, 35 and 36

the masters of bygone days; while among the living men he had perhaps the closest personal contact with the painter Fra Bartolomeo (1475–1517), who had fully mastered the Cinquecento idea of monumental quality, even if his sense of individualised expressive form was utterly defective. Thus equipped, Raphael rose to his chance in Rome, in 1508, when Pope Julius II, Michelangelo's patron, commissioned him to paint a number of frescoes in some halls in the Vatican, known as the *Stanze*. It is these paintings on the basis of which Raphael should above all be judged, showing as they do a really marvellous balance and harmonious development of varied artistic qualities.

Certain of these frescoes should be instanced as specially significant. The earliest of them is the *Disputà* †—an assembly of theologians, with a vision of Heaven above. The dominant motifs of the composition are two large curves formed by the Heavenly and earthly congregations, the latter with marvellous richness of undulations, the former more severe and simple, and the two most beautifully harmonised with one another. In the lower half of the composition is seen a very close adoption of the principles of composition in Leonardo's picture of *The Adoration of the Magi*: the centre of the composition is moved some way back, with a clear space in front and diagonals leading straight to it from each corner; towards the sides there are pillar-like standing figures against which the waves of movement break. The pupil of Perugino is clearly seen in the spaciousness of effect, the soft undulations of the distant hills and the pure sky against which the figures are silhouetted, all motifs of the utmost importance in conveying that reposeful and majestic feeling of which the whole is so beautifully expressive. We have here a most typical instance of the way in which Raphael sums up the efforts of previous artists, impressing, however, the stamp of his own individuality on the whole.

On the wall opposite is the fresco devoted, by contrast, to Theology, to secular learning, philosophy and science: it is popularly known under the name of *The School of Athens*.† The setting for it is designed as a spacious hall in the most noble and monumental style of the Renaissance, opening under a succession of arcades towards the sky—a motif which is connected with a favourite one of Perugino's. In accordance with the diversified nature of scientific research, there is here no convergence of lines and feelings towards a central point, as in the *Disputà*; but the whole is effectively and significantly dominated by the figures of the two great philosophers of classical antiquity, Plato and Aristotle, standing in the centre above, silhouetted against the background of sky, and enclosed by the arch in the distance. The composition is a masterpiece of large and free distribution of groups united to an absolute coherence and lucidity of design.

In another hall in the *Stanze* the subjects of the frescoes are historical, and if in the reposeful and contemplative feeling which marks the frescoes first analysed Raphael's connection with Perugino is typified, he appears in these later ones pre-eminently as continuing the great dramatic traditions of Florentine art—the traditions of Giotto, Masaccio, Donatello and Leonardo. There is also in these frescoes an advance towards a more pictorial style, greater freedom of handling and richer effects of light and shade. Special importance attaches to the frescoes known as *The Mass of Bolsena*—which contains some of the finest passages of actual painting in Raphael's whole work—and *The Expulsion of Heliodorus*, which has links of special interest with the art of Donatello.

Works such as these frescoes in the *Stanze* certainly establish Raphael's rank among the world's great artists; and they also form an integral part of the artistic tradition which every true European carries with him.

† Plate 34

† Plate 35

Plate 4

VISION OF A KNIGHT *by Raphael* (1483-1520)

Original 7″ square

BIBLIOGRAPHY

BERENSON, BERNHARD
Italian Painters of the Renaissance (Oxford, 1930).
Italian Pictures of the Renaissance (Oxford, 1932).
Drawings of the Florentine Painters (London, 1903 ; second edition, Chicago, 1939).

BORENIUS, TANCRED *
Florentine Frescoes (London, 1930).

CLARK, SIR KENNETH
Leonardo da Vinci (Cambridge, 1940).

CROWE, J. A. and CAVALCASELLE, G. B.
A History of Painting in Italy (6 vols. new edition. Vols. I–IV edited by Langton Douglas ; vols. V–VI edited by Tancred Borenius. London, 1903–1914).
A History of Painting in North Italy (3 vols. edited by Tancred Borenius. London, 1912).
Raphael (London, 1884–1885).

FRY, ROGER
Giovanni Bellini (London, 1899).

HORNE, HERBERT P.
Alessandro Filipepi, commonly called Botticelli (London, 1908).

" KLASSIKER DER KUNST " Series
Volumes on *Raphael, Michelangelo, Mantegna, Fra Angelico, Perugino, Signorelli* and *Giovanni Bellini* (Stuttgart).

MARLE, R. VAN
The Development of the Italian Schools of Painting (19 vols. Martinus Nijhoff, The Hague, 1923–1938).

MORELLI, GIOVANNI
Italian Painters (2 vols. London, 1892–1893).

OFFNER, RICHARD
A Critical and Historical Corpus of Florentine Painting (New York, in progress, 1930–   ).

PHAIDON PRESS Series
Volumes on *Michelangelo, Donatello, Raphael, Leonardo, Bellini* (London, 1940–1944).

POPHAM, A. E. (Editor)
The Drawings of Leonardo da Vinci (London, 1946).

SIREN, OSVALD
Giotto and some of his Followers (2 vols. Cambridge, Mass., 1917).
Leonardo da Vinci (London, 1916. Revised French edition, 3 vols. Paris and Brussels, 1928).

YASHIRO, YUKIO
Sandro Botticelli (London, 1929).

* SOME OTHER WORKS BY TANCRED BORENIUS

The Painters of Vicenza, 1909 (also in Italian, 1912).
New editions of *Crowe and Cavalcaselle's History of Painting in Italy,* 1912 and 1914.
Pictures by Old Masters, Library of Christ Church, Oxford, 1916.
Four Early Italian Engravers, 1923.   *English Primitives,* 1924.   *Forty London Statues,* 1926.
English Medieval Painting, 1927 (with Prof. E. W. Tristram ; also in German).
Memorial Volume on Flemish Exhibition (Burlington House, 1927).
English Painting of the XVIIIth Century, 1938 (also in French).   *Rembrandt Paintings,* 1942.

CHRONOLOGICAL LIST

Niccolo Pisano, c. 1205–1278
Cimabue, 1240 ?–after 1302
Giovanni Pisano, c. 1245–c. 1315
Duccio di Buoninsigna, c. 1260–1319
Giotto, 1266/76–1337
Pietro Lorenzetti, c. 1280–c. 1348
Simone Martini, c. 1284–1344
Bernardo Daddi, c. 1290–1348
Andrea Bonaiuti, working early 14th century
Ambrogio Lorenzetti, working 1323–1348
Taddeo Gaddi, c. 1300–1363/66
Maso, c. 1324–c. 1351
Agnolo Gaddi, c. 1333–1396
Don Lorenzo Monaco, c. 1370–c. 1425
Filippo Brunellesco, 1377–1446
Lorenzo Ghiberti, 1378–1455
Masolino, 1383–1447
Donatello, 1386–1466
Fra Angelico, 1387–1455
Gentile da Fabriano, c. 1390–1427
Sassetta, 1392–1450
Altichiero, working end 14th century
Jacopo Avanzo, working end 14th century
Antonio Pisano—called Pisanello, c. 1395–c. 1455
Jacopo Bellini, c. 1395–1470
Francesco Squarcione, 1397–c. 1470
Paolo Uccello, 1397 ?–1475
Masaccio, 1401–1428/29
Giovanni di Paolo, 1403–1482
Fra Filippo Lippi, 1406 ?–1469
Andrea del Castagno, 1410–1457

Piero della Francesca, 1416 ?–1498
Benozzo Gozzoli, 1420–1497
Cosimo Tura, 1420 ?–1496
Francesco Pesellino, 1422–1457
Alesso Baldovinetti, 1425–1499
Gentile Bellini 1429 ?–1507
Giovanni Bellini, c. 1430–1516
Antonello da Messina, c. 1430–1479
Andrea Mantegna, c. 1431–1506
Antonio del Pollaiuolo, 1433–1498
Andrea del Verrocchio, 1435–1488
Matteo di Giovanni, c. 1435–1495
Francesco del Cossa, 1435 ?–1477
Melozzo da Forli, 1438–1494
Francesco di Giorgio, c. 1439–1502
Sandro Botticelli, 1444–1510
Pietro Perugino, c. 1446–1523
Domenico Ghirlandaio, 1449–1494
Domenico Veneziano, working 1450–1461
Luca Signorelli, c. 1450–1523
Ercole de Roberti, 1450 ?–1496
Leonardo da Vinci, 1452–1519
Bernardino Pinturicchio, c. 1454–1514
Filippino Lippi, 1457–1504
Cima da Conegliano, c. 1460–1517/18
Vittore Carpaccio, c. 1460–c. 1525
Piero di Cosimo, 1462–1521
Michelangelo Buonarroti, 1475–1564
Fra Bartolomeo, 1475–1517
Giorgione, c. 1477–1510
Raphael, 1483–1520

ACKNOWLEDGMENT is made to Anderson for valuable assistance in the provision of photographic prints for Plates 5, 6, 7, 10, 13, 16, 20, 22, 25, 26, 30, 32, 33, 34, 35 and 36. Plates 14, 15 and 19 were supplied by W. F. Mansell, and 11, 18 and 27 by Alinari. Plates 8 and 23 were obtained from Rischgitz; Plates 28 and 29 from Giraudon, and Plate 31 from the Warburg Institute. Plate 12 is from a Bruckmann photograph. Colour Plate 1 is reproduced by permission of Messrs. T. C. and E. C. Jack.

LIST OF PLATES

IN COLOUR

THE LAMENTATION OVER THE DEAD CHRIST *By Giotto*	Arena Chapel, Padua	*Frontispiece*
MARS AND VENUS *By Sandro Botticelli*	National Gallery, London	*Plate* 2
VIRGIN AND CHILD *By Filippino Lippi*	Wernher Collection, London	„ 3
VISION OF A KNIGHT *By Raphael*	National Gallery, London	„ 4

IN MONOCHROME (Photogravure)

ST. FRANCIS SUBMITTED TO THE ORDEAL BY FIRE *By Giotto*	Upper Church, S. Francesco, Assisi	„ 5
THE MARRIAGE AT CANA *By Giotto.* Detail	Arena Chapel, Padua	„ 6
THE DREAM OF ST. MARTIN *By Simone Martini*	Lower Church, Assisi	„ 7
THE VISION OF ST. EUSTACE *By Antonio Pisano—called Pisanello*	National Gallery, London	„ 8
THE ROUT OF SAN ROMANO *By Paolo Uccello*	National Gallery, London	„ 9
CORONATION OF THE VIRGIN *By Fra Angelico*	Monastery of S. Marco, Florence	„ 10
EXPULSION FROM PARADISE *By Masaccio*	S. Maria del Carmine, Florence	„ 11
ADORATION OF THE INFANT *By Filippo Lippi*	Kaiser Friedrich Museum, Berlin	„ 12
THE RESURRECTION *By Piero della Francesca*	Town Hall, Borgo San Sepolcro	„ 13
THE MADONNA *By Cosimo Tura*	National Gallery, London	„ 14
THE MADONNA AND CHILD *By Alesso Baldovinetti*	Louvre, Paris	„ 15
THE MIRACLE OF THE HOLY CROSS *By Gentile Bellini*	R. Accademia, Venice	„ 16
THE AGONY IN THE GARDEN *By Giovanni Bellini*	National Gallery, London	„ 17
THE LAST SUPPER *By Andrea del Castagno*	Monastery of S. Apollonia, Florence	„ 18
THE BIRTH OF ST. JOHN THE BAPTIST *By Domenico Ghirlandaio*	S. Maria Novella, Florence	„ 19
THE TRIAL OF ST. JAMES *By Andrea Mantegna*	Church of the Hermits, Padua	„ 20
THE MADONNA ADORING THE CHILD *By Pietro Perugino.* Central Panel of a Triptych	National Gallery, London	„ 21
HERCULES AND THE HYDRA *By Antonio del Pollaiuolo*	Uffizi Gallery, Florence	„ 22
ANGEL : detail from THE ASCENSION *By Melozzo da Forli*	Vatican Gallery, Rome	„ 23
DEATH OF PROCRIS *By Piero di Cosimo*	National Gallery, London	„ 24
PRIMAVERA *By Sandro Botticelli*	Uffizi Gallery, Florence	„ 25
THE MADONNA APPEARING TO ST. BERNARD *By Filippino Lippi*	Church of the Badia, Florence	„ 26
THE ADORATION OF THE MAGI *By Leonardo da Vinci*	Uffizi Gallery, Florence	„ 27
MONA LISA *By Leonardo da Vinci*	Louvre, Paris	„ 28
THE VIRGIN OF THE ROCKS *By Leonardo da Vinci*	Louvre, Paris	„ 29
THE MADONNA AND CHILD ENTHRONED *By Giorgione*	Cathedral, Castelfranco	„ 30
GIORGIONE'S FAMILY *By Giorgione*	R. Accademia, Venice	„ 31
THE CREATION OF MAN *By Michelangelo Buonarroti*	Sistine Chapel, Vatican, Rome	„ 32
THE ORIGINAL SIN *By Michelangelo Buonarroti*	Sistine Chapel, Vatican, Rome	„ 33
DISPUTÀ *By Raphael*	Stanze, Vatican, Rome	„ 34
THE SCHOOL OF ATHENS *By Raphael*	Stanze, Vatican, Rome	„ 35
THE MARRIAGE OF THE MADONNA *By Raphael*	Brera Gallery, Milan	„ 36

Plate 5

St. FRANCIS SUBMITTED TO THE ORDEAL BY FIRE *By Giotto* (1266/76-1337)

Fresco

THE MARRIAGE AT CANA *By Giotto* (1266/76-1337)

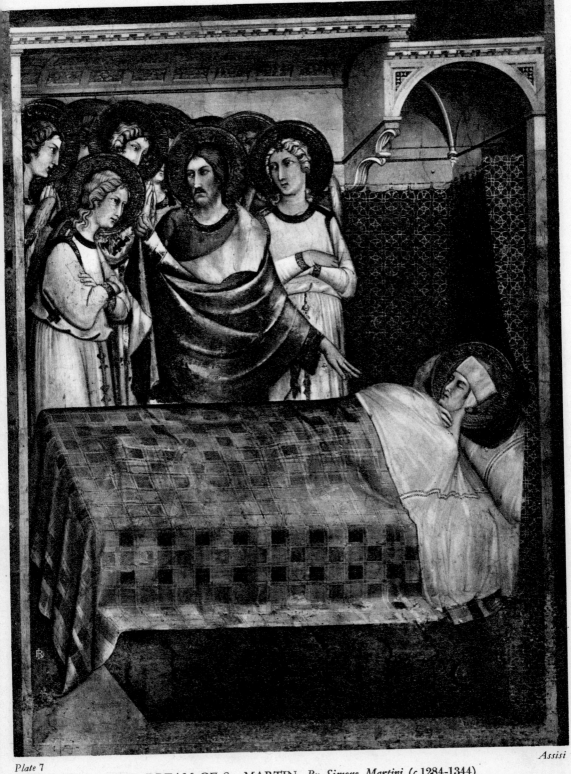

Plate 7

THE DREAM OF St. MARTIN *By Simone Martini (c.1284-1344)*

Fresco

Plate 8   THE VISION OF St. EUSTACE By Antonio Pisano, called Pisanello

Plate 9

THE ROUT OF SAN ROMANO *By Paolo Uccello (c.1397-1475)*

Wood 72" × 125"

Plate 10

Florence

CORONATION OF THE VIRGIN *By Fra Angelico* (1387-1455)

Fresco 74½″ × 62½″

Plate 11   *Florence*

EXPULSION FROM PARADISE *By Masaccio* (1401-1428/29)

Fresco

ADORATION OF THE INFANT *By Fra Filippo Lippi (1406?-1469)*

Borgo San Sepolcro

THE RESURRECTION *By Piero della Francesca* (1416?-1498)

Plate 14

THE MADONNA *By Cosimo Tura* (1420?-1496)

Wood 17½″ × 13″

Plate 15

THE MADONNA AND CHILD *By Alesso Baldovinetti* (1425-1499)

Canvas 50" × 30"

THE MIRACLE OF THE HOLY CROSS

Plate 16

Plate 17

THE AGONY IN THE GARDEN. By *Giovanni Bellini.* (*c.*1430–1516)

Wood 32″ × 50″

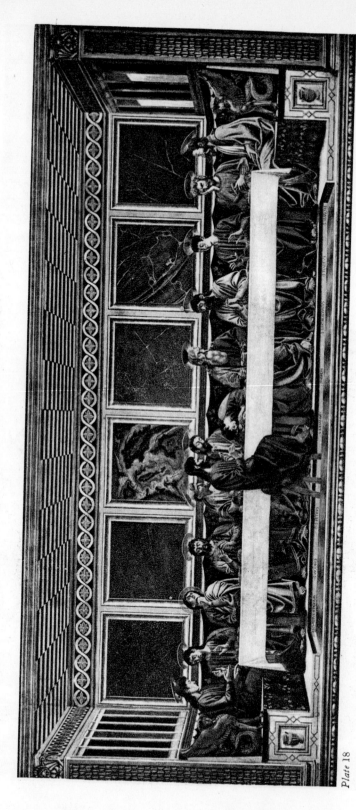

Plate 18

THE LAST SUPPER *By Andrea del Castagno (1410-1457)*

Fresco

Florence

THE BIRTH OF St. JOHN THE BAPTIST *By Domenico Ghirlandaio* (1449-1494)

Plate 19

Plate 20

THE TRIAL OF St. JAMES *By Andrea Mantegna (c.1431-1506)*

Padua

Fresco

Plate 21   *National Gallery*

THE MADONNA ADORING THE CHILD *By Pietro Perugino (c.1446-1523)*

Wood 50"x 25½"   Central Panel of a Triptych.

HERCULES AND THE HYDRA *By Antonio del Pollaiuolo* (1433-1498)

Wood 6⅝″ × 4¾″

Plate 23

Rome

ANGEL : detail from THE ASCENSION *By Melozzo da Forli* (1438-1494)

Fresco (fragment)

DEATH OF PROCRIS *By Piero di Cosimo (1462-1521)*

Plate 24

Wood 25½" × 72"

Plate 25

PRIMAVERA By Sandro Botticelli (1444-1510)

Wood 80"x123½"

Plate 26

Florence

THE MADONNA APPEARING TO St. BERNARD   *By Filippino Lippi* (1457-1504)

Wood

Plate 27

THE ADORATION OF THE MAGI *By Leonardo da Vinci (1452-1519)*

Wood 97″ × 95½″

Plate 28

Wood 30¼" × 21"

MONA LISA *By Leonardo da Vinci* (1452-1519)

Louvre

Plate 29

THE VIRGIN OF THE ROCKS *By Leonardo da Vinci* (1452-1519)

Canvas 78" × 48½"

Plate 30

Castelfranco

THE MADONNA AND CHILD ENTHRONED *By Giorgione (c.1477-1510)*

Panel 78¾″ × 59⅞″

Plate 31

GIORGIONE'S FAMILY *By Giorgione (c.1477-1510)*

Canvas 30" × 28½"

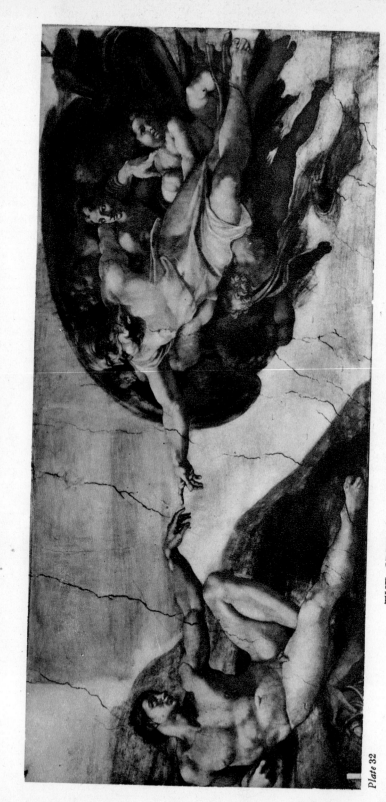

Plate 32

Fresco

THE CREATION OF MAN *By Michelangelo Buonarroti (1475-1564)*

Sistine Chapel, Rome

Plate 33

Sistine Chapel, Rome

THE ORIGINAL SIN By *Michelangelo Buonarroti* (1475-1564)

Fresco

DISPUTÀ *By Raphael* (1483-1520)

Plate 34

Fresco

Rome

THE SCHOOL OF ATHENS *By Raphael* (1483-1520)

Plate 35

Plate 36

THE MARRIAGE OF THE MADONNA *By Raphael (1483-1520)*